Life in Transition

Grayson DeLeon

BookLeaf
Publishing

India | USA | UK

Presentation by *BookLeaf Publishing*

Web: www.bookleafpub.com

E-mail: info@bookleafpub.com

ISBN: 9789363306394

First edition 2024

For anyone who has taken the time to read, an expression of negative emotion is not defeatist, so let yourself feel.

ACKNOWLEDGEMENT

I would like to thank the following in no particular order. In thanks to my parents for their love and support, my brother for being just that. To the people who make me feel the most at home, a world of love to my stand partner (formerly), Kolet, my truest friend, and all my long-term friendships who have witnessed my growth. I am grateful to the teacher in room 117 for inspiration and advice, and those friend's families who celebrate my milestones. To every adult, non-adult, and mentor figure alike who has held space for me to be seen and heard, (and for talking about Buffy the Vampire Slayer with me), thank you from the bottom of my heart. It feels strange to mention each one in gratitude rather than in a goodbye, but I am beyond appreciative for that fact alone. And as always, thank you to my old coach, without whom I would not have found pride in my existence.

PREFACE

"I lost part of myself,
I gave so much away"
was it out of kindness?
"Yes"
Then all you did was allow a little more
kindness in the world if only temporary.

Could You Understand

I think the ocean spends all day trying to reach
the sky.
It's desperate and tried formation of waves
over and over,
extending their height
Each attempt destined to crash and plummet
catastrophically,
The ocean's most painful failure is casually
beautiful.
and in the same way each has its depths, still
they do not reach.
Forbidden to touch.
The ocean angers,
from being so withdrawn,
so burdened, with reflecting what is longed for
on its surface.
So close yet so deafeningly far.
perhaps we ought to forgive hurricanes and
tsunamis.
(that may be a stretch)
A wave crests and falls,
condemned to return to the single connected
mass that is the ocean.
Days spent waiting for nightfall
when its singularity is less a curse

There is strength in waiting.
For when darkness is in succession,
there is no separation between the shifting
surface of the seas,
and the horizon's entryway to the sky
Whitewash and Stars.
That is why, we are not allowed.
given no light no credence
The darkened waters need time with its other,
just as you or I.
And when the weightlessness of space can no
longer sustain a dying star,
the ocean will extend once more and carry its
stardust to the sand.
home by means of nature
I think the ocean knows us all

Skittish is my friend Paranoia

Paranoia clambers up the pathway to distortion.
settles in.
stilling reason
stilling time
was it ever still?
the pattern of my silhouette
Abjectly horrible
in the way it rattles,
echoes along
a low rumbling at the opening of a long descent
to madness
breath barely caught.
Intrinsic is the shadowed outline at a glance
my pirouetting silhouette

my mind had toppled- a cracked weight
left behind where the rocks tower endlessly
centuries streaked on their surface
years streaked on my skin
rubbed raw
from
Paranoia.
Paranoia and her assailants
a murmuration of worries,
tearing at the seams

the very fabrication of what is accustomed.
I hear it calling,
A broken staircase
Paranoia
Is my mind's art,
I make it with my hands every day
further from the place I was
contrary to the ebb and
flow of feeling,
since discontinuing
a narrative that of which, I am not
I cannot shake this
incessant,
creeping,
Paranoia.

The Shock of Summer Stays the Same

I find myself on Summer days,
Indisposed
Needless to say I do not find myself at all.
the Sun makes a wisecrack of the wind
and
Summer's heat seeps thickly
into my figure
I know it.
Hummingbirds must be figments of the
imagination
For they usually seem to vanish,
evaporated upon second glance.
Reaching inward for strength in Summer
is like
chasing a hummingbird.

Condensation on soda cans
remind me of the way I often felt chagrined
as a child
Always a feeling
never a why
always an absence
Never of what
I am lucky it has not always been so dominant.

I romanticize Summer as to not feel so exposed,
so as to not feel so intensely,
as to not feel.
I wonder at the lifespan of a worm
The concrete starkly too hot for survival
Too hot for survival-
I do not have to wonder.

The heat migrates south for the Winter.
No, those are the birds. that is Winter
this is wrongly
Summer
Still.
The heat migrates somewhere beneath my
breasts
Pushing out,
I never see snails anymore
Forcing extension,
or perhaps I stopped paying attention.
temperature sings hidden insecurities,
a facade of gleefulness
Crumbles
I could mold anthills with.

Too hot for survival.
too hot for survival,
No.
And no one knows but they do, don't they?

They must
must sense
the impending crash of solace burning out.
must also see
The betrayal of my discernible figure.
Except that is just
the Summer heat
And those would attest, I have never had heat
stroke.

Discomfort finds me in odd places though its
presence is never odd
I imagine being born is something of a
discomfort.
Do Hummingbirds fly south?
I was born
A hummingbird would die trying southwards.
I was born,
midst a 2005 July
And the disturbance in season of swelter
stays the same
Agonizing.
A forcible reentry of my emergence
Every Summer I am reborn.
How else to explain the shock.

Little Red Lines

Like an emptiness not yet empty,
Time fills in what I cannot on my own
Like the burgeoning of an actor,
My performance speaks, so I do not have to.
Like the swallowed vision of an eclipse,
My mind tires like the sun
The thought of standstill swells and plunges
In deep descent
Inchoate.
It's fair to say, I'm young.
An emptiness not yet empty,
I pour out confessions of truth
I myself,
An anachronism
In the spiraling tendrils of daily stupor.
Like the spasming of indecision,
My presence wavers like the tide
Pupils widening out the entrance
to a dilettante little life
Overbearing,
Scattered vocation,
In a demeanor like accepted fate.
Dispelling the overwhelming sense of metal
Unremarkably,
consolation follows suit.

Dependency bleeds red
And I run my inflictions
through and through,
as deep ingrained the habits,
of outpouring degenerative harm
My universal solvent.
My storage of shame.
Deeds,
as misplaced care
a fixation, a fix
that thrives in puddles of penance
Like an emptiness not yet empty,
I dance around my words
the fleeting rush of inditement.
Of affliction.
The release of pent-up hurt.
I exhaust the desolate landscape of my arms,
reimagined canvas
Apply pressure to halt continuance.
I strain my worth,
I keep my change
Do I encompass the space I fill?
I hover in the emptiness, not fully emptied,
Not fully formed
Not fully living.
This is the aching of my actions
Raised little blips.

Some Days it is Easier Not to

I do not think
I have ever encountered myself the same way
that people do.
I have never met
the girl that one stop cashier rung up at the
grocery store,
The curious boy-girl
that mother eyed away from her child in a lonely
aisle
The gray one-day happiness, to the three letter
love of an old name the next.
If nothing ever
points toward me consistently,
haven't I achieved all constrictions I reject?
An old man met a young boy at a coffee shop
the same time I was there
I know because he stood soundly
Or wasn't I
"It's nice to see you again"
See me where?
Me where I'm wearing me or the me I wear in
openness?
I have yet to relearn how to sign my name.
I think understanding only follows,
after a difficult confrontation with pain.

"young lady"
"how may I help you?"
I wasn't aware there was one here
to help
"How may I help you?"
But she needs it, doesn't she.
The tampons? I ask
Upstairs.
Up stares and downstairs
Staring after someone
who does not exist.
There is relief,
in fulfilling wrongful assumption
under the guise of avoiding disturbance.
But don't I?
Doesn't he?
Doesn't she raise that itself
Liberation
Each elusive shift into them-ness
A proper word, hardly
but it exists more than she does.
They collected change
a receipt
They smiled,
held a door
He stumbled in recognition,
Him,
radiant in ephemeral blindness,
They took free space as free space

I don't always remember,
It's not always me
But I was there.

Birthdays- "Happy birthday to you" (There's so little left of me)

My heart
tears in two
Its seams are stitches I cannot mend
I cannot mend.
for on this night, midnight,
and some dreadful 52 minutes
there goes my youth.
and my heart
my heart
struggles to find a way back to sensibility.
Freedom with no legs to run on
I feel inconclusive.
harp,
quicken the process of the ever beating organ
ripped in two, for I am two
forever two
of me.
veins coursing, pumping,
steady like the water faucet left on
My veins run on accidents and each trickle of
blood cascades with no choice
no reason

flippant as it is drawn out
between the coiled bridging seams
of my heart
My heart ripping further than two
too mangled, too pulverized
Age shouts in my ear.
ricochets, tumbles blindly,
down the tunnel of a dimly lit eardrum
a hollow sound
Is the sound of childhood,
thudding as it hits an empty stomach
Follow the dotted line.
Threads shrivel,
tearing, as time approaches midnight and some
dreadful minutes más
What will I do when it finally rips?
I thought I was two
of me
already
I thought I could live in me as her
I feel her.
My first heart
Her outstretched limbs throbbing,
her blood dissolving the threads holding together
my present.
her ever so revolving past.
fingers melting, eroding, disjointed like wax
disfigured.
red spiteful wax to encase what's left.

What's left?
Of my youth?

By the time that I am old,
If I am ever old
what will be left?
of that flitting little girl
Washed away in her own bloodstream

For Love, Not Together is Not Halting Enough/Go Forth With Mine Eternally

"I Love you"
"I love You"
I love you is not always kind to poor
circumstance.
"I'm sorry"
"I'm sorry."
apologies
do not ease mutual sacrifice.
"I miss you"
"I Miss you."
A synonym for this hurts me.
I love you.
I wish you didn't.
don't say that.
I'm sorry.
"Are you okay?"
"Define okay"
Okay,
I love you.
"I Love You."
Love withstanding wields means to divaricate.
Is this what you want?

of course?
I'm sorry.
I love you.
"We work
we're okay.
okay?"
"Okay."
if it doesn't it will break me.
if it doesn't
If it doesn't it will change me
It doesn't.
"I Love You.

I love you"
?

Prescription Suppression

Spitting out words,
or nearly
spitting out words
Gibberish prefaces my ruination
An imminent encounter with the stupored face I
hide
Deep-rooted tears
deep-rooted tears
Melt white-hot on my eyelids.
Shut with fake sleep when time approaches near,
Opened again
only to find the wisps of my hair tethering to the
mangled face.
The face that hides.
Closed.
"Here I am"
tinkers a laugh
Take me take me take me
Entrap me here and I'll chase it into oblivion.
there are things to be forgotten,
Humanness
Discarded,
For the much estranged moment.
Moments measured by bleariness
At the corners of my vision

My vision or my pulse.
As two lines on a face stretch wider,
Don't make me think too much,
for thoughts are the reason the sky falls down
every day.
"Don't you see? Don't you see?"
The insipid white-hot seethed through my
retinas
I bathe in it,
         Thank it,
Because it brought me here
To the nook where I do not
exist
To anybody, nobody
No body
The wondrous (dangerous) void of
Nothing
         until everything under suppression
returns
(and it does)
Think I'd want to be
I don't want to be
The face that hides.

Nothing Ever Happens on Sunday Mornings

I rode the train in my mind this morning.
Took direction as a suggestion to declutter the
stacks,
the books
Leaflets
I let three stops go by before getting off.
And would the world look different if you
looked down to see your heels?
Mine stood
at the edge of the platform,
but all in sight were my toes.
"Don't stand so close"
I forgot a ladder I say
What for? your toes don't hold the answers.
The books
the titles I cannot reach,
I came to declutter
The next train boards.

Dazed and confused
when did my feet reunite themselves here?
I check,
not backwards.
Jump

turn
face the end of the train car
papers barreling fast
My clutter knocks me over, and I lie dead on the
carpeted floor.
"Look at the ink"
a hand plunges
through my nose
a finger,
my arm
the sole of one's foot,
my leg
People leaving their seats,
I am everywhere.
I must reshelve A-Z

The train stops.

Consume me

Perhaps
Intellect,
mirrors pigmentation
from obstruction of youth to teenaged skin.
The lengthening of limbs into fuller distinction
the muscle memory of right from wrong.
Consume me

Perhaps
Security,
is woven through achievement.
perfection in imperfection,
a separation from upheld quotidian
Connected by means of intellect.
you fall
I stand
you stand
I run
I speak
you comment
competition unspoken.
To be taken in by the target of attachment is to
be the best.
Consume me

Perhaps
Control,
starts at one's core.
Spreads like disease through the limbs
Halting growth- but control.
I have control
Progresses rapidly, it impedes
Seizing in the rib cage, the sensation of two
magnets,
facing their like poles
Intellect repelled from the brain,
an imbalance in the head
faint.
An empty torso,
an emptied person
Shaking, uncontrollable,
Control
Cope
the weakness that follows
the inanition that gnaws,
collapses function
disguises wrongs in the body, causes wrongs in
the body,
I have it.
Under.
Control.

Perhaps
Revival,

argues achievement with intellect
Once putrescence reversed
Offers recovery in lieu of control.
reminds one of limbs of a fuller distinction,
Prompts readiness,
Subserves living.

Control
Achievement
Security
Intellect
control,
Competition
Control
Consume me,
(Release me)
Consume me. Release me.
in emaciation of flesh and intellect,
in deterioration of corpus and personality
I insist.

It is like asking me
to kill an angel
And go behind a demon's back.

Familiarity Chases the Mind on a Precipice

I paint gloom in December
The unintentional fog that skims all sunken
corners
plastered grins
Liquified in the burnt– it gets dark early sky,
take me this time skies
And it was sad they'll admit
but it's sad the way the air stills.
glow of a light left on
It exists in the withering
the gradients
On a softly shadowed wall
outlines so familiar mine buckle.
The walls
They catch me whispering.
night after night after night after
It's the use of tinted orange in nostalgia,
watercolors for gray blue hues
Seeping
blanketed
Unkept hours tucked in the crook of my
shoulder,
I feel for my bones

I have never seen the same thing I wanted to again.

Be Calm Be Still

I tried to sleep naked in the bedroom
only to discern my instincts clothed,
a resolute objection to vulnerability
this space a gatekeeper of birthright.

The bear sits softly in the corner,
her eyes bright as polished stone
Repose comes easy to body of cotton.
A window collects hoots of owl,
stored in closed nightshades
And I feel
ever known

To topple the grass that lies atop bedchambers
the crickets lose sleep
Do they not,
chirp
their symphony lifts vigilance from eyes,
Do not stir.

Happier dreams a folly sundown,
sunup, the pleasant surprise of none
The absence of treats the body the same.
thin streams of light,
an out pour of new arrival

If not I, somewhere

Day life constellates the green and brown,
the lawns, the roads, returned to fall mire
An abundance of creature time hidden
Kind, be kind

The opened sky here less open
Human impudence, the leading lady to such
caliginous affairs.
Light closes its daily chapter,
One last swim, crawl, flight
kiss, song, chatter
Let the sun end its dance across the blue bled
gloaming.
Dusk life resumes,
starts small,
Duets of sound, the startling rustle
My window waits for the owl.

I tried to sleep laid bare
I tried to sleep.
ribbons of thought trailed to the cloisters above
Naked emotion– concupiscible
El grillo sings

I adjure the darkness for movement in sleep,
I await the soothing of synchronous sound to
evade incubus,

I await.
and sink,
Gasping for breath
into the arms of ardent longing
The cotton bodies know.
May respite blanket my being tonight.

Memento Mori

Encased
is the person who so desperately desires
fulfillment, I cannot provide as I am.
An effort to render and yet,
Encased is myself still.
In a timeless body my mind does not recognize
as its own.
I plead for release of this prison I have grown
into

I plead for absolution
I plead for my life.

In a garden, I still.
Mishappen body forgotten in the thrawn of two
person steps
I do not sense
my slight grotesqueness to my frame,
the opened wounds of last night.
The ache in my back,
nor the tightened cords to my chest.
In this way you ease the deepest part of my pain.

I thank you.

"I just got home"

I collapse what I was born as
and feel it crash down onto who I am, and in that
second I miss what is not my own

adjust a ring,
I seek out the faint metronome of the comfort I
find
in us
and trust
I am seen.
I am seen by you.

It hurts where it hurts, and I face my time as I
am meant
In the broken solitude of my own flesh and
blood.
Mine. Belonging to me.
Not mine, I swear.
Am I not suited for self-love?
Envelop me with you in embrace and hide my
body from me please.

I trust you
alone
to truly not see
my present figure.
I trust myself, to let go of violent concentrations,
of subtle movement and space I hold.

We are compositions of everything we have seen
come to pass,
and if temporal form is what enables poetry,
let your company enable peace.

let your company enable peace in me
let your company enable peace in me.

Items and interests collected, continuously wane
as nature sees fit.
I place trust that all I am
may live un-indebted to pain in your eyes
In your memory as time allows.

Memento mori-
Remember, you must die.

My remembrance– often turned to dutiful
attempts
A preemptive disruption of
a cadence between two people who know.
A rarity.
a chance at diversive joy
Be not abstracted
I ever so yearned.
I have tried two times over,
I try no longer

If I must it won't be soon.

Chance: A Ten Step Guide

1. Decision requires completion. Preparation,
corrosion of the greatest event
Opportunity feeds desperation. Secret, keep a
secret,
Commence.

2. A collection of small healers, my apologies
for misuse. Subjection measured in milligrams,
purpose: pain reliever.

3. Reassess, read the label, reassess
I am unable to feel the weight of conviction. A
single-minded station with a single-minded goal
In searching for hope I enervate its vitality.
Warning: Do not take more than directed.

4. Swallow. Enrapture the senses, let fear stain
the air I breathe
The intake of toxicity, a superposition of what
anguish seeks shelter from.
Inhale, let it, swallow.
In enduring, my alertness will devastate me.

5. Sickness, ill of body, a rotation of mind and
soul, what takes? what gives?

Is it more fool hearted to pursue a flailing end or
rip free the foible root?

6. Uses: temporarily relives minor aches
and pains
due to:
The common burnout
Headache
Muscular collapse
Minor pain of exposure to indefinite pain.
Temporary, swallow. Pain, swallow, swallow.
Temporary, swallow.

7. Temporary
Cleansing
Once more, permanent.

8. A trial of waiting emanates a lifetime of
undulated misery.
Symptoms: skin discoloration, nausea, agitation,
sufferance.

9. Abide the passage of time, submit longing
into bedsheets,
Submit.

10. Prolonged discontinuance, not sinless
A volatile eruption of body fighting intention.
I hurl chance from my intestines,

disposing the idea of permanent relief
A bodily reminder, once more,
You cannot be rid of me.

The failed evasion of working cells,
Bind down emotion,
Stuck
with the stench of outcome in the air
And so it begins again.

It All Comes Back in the End (There is more of me left than it seemed)

There is a tragedy in time and permanence
Suspect
And I will never tell the aspect of which is more
soothing
Most horrific in its nature
Moreover,
I have breached my stagnancy
Of each
It seems
idling.
For dismissive of age,
For expectation of age,
I age in eleven days time and I long for
forgetfulness
or consumption.
16
15
14
18 and I remember
13
Sincere is best descriptive of their summation.
Or rather the nearest replacement for pain.

17 remains amiss.
My becoming,
nothing short of
excruciating
A liveliness awakened,
from
a mind plagued torment.
I shed fear,
from every soft corner of my personhood
Over the thread bound,
one's death, and my wake
and still, I change.
Rise in the taking,
Overt torrents of memory
My soul cradles each comforting sign.
For 6 years of displacement,
searing,
and severed connection
Would you know me now?
There is a tragedy and there is a loss of great
reward
The select few,
I, a part,
in asking for promise of resurrection.
You must ask,
in time
in permanence
Of which speaks the limit you are willing to
forgive

and one day,
Someday, I will see you tomorrow.

The First Man to Love

I think you'd like the way my skin cracked
from your pressure beneath me
It's strange how,
You will never notice
until I am old.
Until the cracks you have caused are visible on
my skin with age
and you will have them too,
a myriad
a history a voice cannot tell.
I will know not those that you keep together,
a fair few I will take for my doing.
Even in desolation, I am your defense.

I frequently question whether I will ever be
caught up to you in age
Not old enough, I must have been old enough to
you
When I have been told through my brief
lifetime
"old soul"
still not enough.
without dubiety,
Against my wishes,
For my hopes

I know I will be.

Unduly
I have reached the point of having felt aged,
more than
feeling my age.
for having been, not old enough
Age itself should have meant assurance
shelter
the state of smiling on a rain filled day
I did,
I did
I may have willed myself not to know

I love you so much it's sickening,
beg and I sicken you

Already,
all at once
I am more than I can stand sometimes.

You make my standing seem uncertain
I must have been old enough (young enough) for
you.
The near presence of,
and my joints buckle from the spitting tensity
behind eyes.
I let slip through the cracks on my skin,
You have seen the marks

Littering my arms with their once untamed
duress.
I know I am responsible
I know you have made me so.

In healing they have shrunk.
You have shrunk me
My standing hurts and I am shrinking
Shrinking to recklessly fit into each crack still
left open.
you ought to know they reopen, agape.
To add insult to injury, when added insult and
injury.
I am half unsure if my once youthful openness
was an invitation
For an entering against my will
wishes, will,
the same?
I've decided I don't want to know

Is my deciding the basis of the severed
connection to love?
Do I cut off love at its limbs because I know
yours have hurt mine?
I said I do not want to know.

I fear you
(I said I don't want to know)
but I fear for you more.

And I suspect that will only grow in time
Like the cracks on my skin.
after all
It was only just a surgery.

Hints of Blue on Faded Stucco

A crushing spirit I have never been
And yet with such effect walks just one
To keep routine how ever thin
Her footsteps sound in mourn.

In times of day I see her walk
Always an avoidant gaze
My understanding is none that she has been
taught
But what of I demands her sadness be raised?

Foreground and still, sense her fervent manner
The lonesome man I try to ask
His duty preserves my year ridden glamour
From his cleaning, new shape- tasked is it is she

A scarring on my surface,
A mosaic
a new feeling until,
Caught reflection of a pair
Butterfly wings.

Attention they have brought anew
Suffice to say,

appearance sustains deference
Yet a dreariness is brought into
The silent one, face still askew.
I watch as she goes distantly past
Following her aching
Running from it- how it lasts
I am outstretched, to exhort her ache to bring
But familiarity evades my grasp.

Emptied hallways and I recall
The day she helped bring near
Chalks and stones and gesture of all
Memorial unshed tears.

A week of her absence incites my bereavement
Although I know no such thing
I aim to be
not her grief, not a lingering except
Sadness, how it clings.

Insufferable weakness I know not
For a girl has nothing in common with a wall
And she may retract my claws from her head
An allowance of tile pieces to embed

Run little girl do not come back
I will protect the life you shared
And in the well of dreams you've dreamt
I hope my symbol allows your spirit leisure

to no longer detest
The living dead

Losing a childhood body meant Losing My Home

My chest caves in with every glance in the
mirror
No.
Its Protrusion stirs something in me that I exert
myself to forget–
thoughts engraved throughout the inner walls of
my body
already imprinted.
There is an acute violence in the ways in which I
have judged myself.
Subjected wrongdoings upon innocent
incongruity
Sleep,
Forget

I woke up, mornings tethered in such standard
brush,
Dress,
Eat.
The inner linings of my skin
smooth
untouched
A child in the eyes of the world is simply a
person

underdeveloped
A person.
a body
An entity to grow self discovery from the riches
of non perception
Where did you go?

I woke up,
Hopeful the laws of gravity had exercised their
power overnight.
Crushed the budding evidence of my eventual
womanhood from my home
Rearranged my bones into something more
fitting for a person likened to autonomy.
Instead, an invasion of everything I was taught
should be
Protected
Safety, Security, Peace, Pride
Macerated like the foods used to satiate child
hunger in the stomach
The seeds of guttural distress planted (ignored)
Watered by each wave of nausea turned tsunami
in age.
come back, come back, come back come back

I woke up,
Heartbroken.
Mortification in bloom (ignored)
An admission of the truth,

buried underneath the roots of a swollen exterior
Protrusions kept alive by intumescence

I woke up,
Brokenhearted
I woke up,
Brokenhearted
I made wishes for the end,
Broken.

I have never felt right.
That isn't entirely true
I haven't felt myself since puberty.

every thought
every scratching doubt
each spike of discomfort
every surge of twisting agony has left my
innards bloody and torn
brutally Shredded,
raw

It's my heart that caves in
with every glance in the mirror
Never once my chest.
glimpses in reflections,
myself unrecognizable,
comfort only borrowed,
My home, a vicious war zone

since the halting perception of being
a person.
A person who embodies a human vessel
not one based on
because of
a body born in.
In spite of I am

Would you blame a pained child for missing
home?
I just want back what was mine.

The Farouche Wildflower

fluidity, Power
a delicateness, the color of our

We contain an unyielding essence,
the fuse that sets forth parlous anger, are the
same sparks we dance in

Restorative joy, circumspection, an honesty
dawdle in outrage and love and atrocity

Set forth thinking, question biology,
aged textbooks, California poppies,
the same hue as the sunset o'er mountains

Contained interest as thinking mentions
And dismay and dignity alike,
interconnected, in an addled mind

A woman speaks
in protection, in tone,
similar to a mother wielding knowledge
like a stone

So maims the wildflower, So speaks the mother
So chases the former after the latter

intent to instill understanding,
the other to build
inner doubt cast upon the two, both as one felt

Maturity, femininity, evasiveness, gallantry
And the scorching of the sun and the heat and
the exigency of reality,
expropriate the little plant of its beautiful
obscurity.
A delayed flourishing, a delayed adolescence,
Oh what to become when one loses touch with
essence
A woman it is not,
as much a woman as when uttered
stop.
A wildflower wilts, the search for water
underground,
tunneled passages of harbor,
community set abound

Stout in build, by the sun decides
Masculinity, bravado,
an austere lasting, sentenced,
contrived
With tumored expectation of a white manor
garden.
And seedlings same, pruning de rigeuer,
cross a paragon identical to that of many a
century before.

Becalmed be the lonelier, as a lull courts the
wind
Seeking the derelict phrases of underbrush din
To be seen is to be saved
in which the wildflower grows
An ostentation of formality, no longer kept,
In row

And the wild one sprouts anew, beneath the
shade of it's queer sisters
A robust tangle of effeminate virility
Euphoric
rid of sequester
and safe havened, at long last.

Dear Hands,

Gentle in writing this "Dear"
These hands
the structure of
comes easily,
folds neatly,
with such prose
to have engendered my expression
insistently malicious,
but out of aegis
to reckon your motive I see,
my inure of that which you keep
in bringing me fellow feeling.

My hands, these hands,
mind's extension of reason,
the medium of ebullient creation.
so I fold to your whims
of fanciful solution within
a burden I pass to you.

For items of which you've kept,
beyond reason of my furtherance
these hands I offer mission
and in them they take to reissue

avoidance,
care,
conviction.

Permission to deepen a graze,
it is okay to graze others like you
for I only came with two
you're okay,
I assure.
Learning, as mind follows cycle
mine, my hands,
I address you,
and I watch you write.

Traverse the page with an endowed blitheness
I am not
surprised.
knowledge breeds emotion and this
I know you recall.
we share the same of each,
and for this, my saying is necessary

I forgive you.

I Will Take Care of Them

He appears sometimes like an apparition.
Like something I've wistfully projected into an
existence,
I only ever catch glimpses of
Flickering in and out.
Some being who holds all aspects of which I
currently cannot possess
Of all that I hope is real,
and not simply
a damaged little girl's imagination illusion
Lost to time and old modern humanity.
In a sense,
They are one conjoined by freedom of form.
For all she had felt but not known is all he
knows to be true
I myself, known to experience blips of truth
whilst normality, tightened the grips of
suffocation.
Truth be told, I am not him
am not yet
But I have carried her within
I have carried her in love,
She has carried me through.
them pulling
just so,

The blurring of us, them. Me
Nothing is the same as nothing ever does
but I have never felt more myself

Grayson you can rest.
She is safe now

www.ingramcontent.com/pod-product-compliance
Lightning Source LLC
La Vergne TN
LVHW021238200726
843509LV00012B/1525